Chiggers

Gail Jarrow

KIDHAVEN PRESS™

THOMSON

━━━━━━✴━━━━━━ ™

GALE

San Diego • Detroit • New York • San Francisco • Cleveland
New Haven, Conn. • Waterville, Maine • London • Munich

THOMSON
GALE

© 2004 by KidHaven Press. KidHaven Press is an imprint of The Gale Group, Inc.,
a division of Thomson Learning, Inc.

KidHaven™ and Thomson Learning™ are trademarks used herein under license.

For more information, contact
KidHaven Press
27500 Drake Rd.
Farmington Hills, MI 48331-3535
Or you can visit our Internet site at http://www.gale.com

LIBRARY OF CONGRESS CATALOGING-IN-PUBLICATION DATA

Jarrow, Gail.
  Chiggers / by Gail Jarrow.
    v. cm. — (Parasites)
Includes bibliographical references and index.
Contents: The chigger: a young mite—Attack on humans—The chigger disease—
Avoiding chigger bites.
  ISBN 0-7377-1778-5 (hardback : alk. paper)
  1. Chiggers (Mites)—Juvenile literature. [1. Chiggers (Mites)] I. Title. II. Series.
RA641.M5J37 2004
616.9'6—dc21
                                          2003009614

CONTENTS

CHAPTER 1

The Chigger—
A Young Mite

Chigger is the common name given to the **larva** of several kinds, or species, of mites. Other names are red bug, harvest mite, and jigger. Mites are **arachnids**, the group of eight-legged animals that also includes spiders, ticks, and scorpions.

Only the mite larvae (chiggers) are parasites. The chiggers must have food from skin cells in order to survive and grow into adult mites. Their usual host is a bird or small mammal. Chiggers sometimes attack snakes, turtles, and frogs.

People may become hosts when they walk through chigger territory.

A chigger looks similar to the eight-legged adult mite, although it is smaller and has only six legs. While the adult mites are usually bright red, chiggers vary in color from creamy white to red. They are covered with tiny hairs.

Their Favorite Places

Chiggers prefer to live close to the ground in damp, shady areas. Favorite spots are on grassy weeds and leaf litter at the edges of woods and water. The creatures are also found in lawns, brush, and berry patches.

Chiggers live throughout the world. In the United States they are more common in the South and Midwest. The parasites are active during warm months.

Chiggers are parasites that feed on skin cells of animals and people.

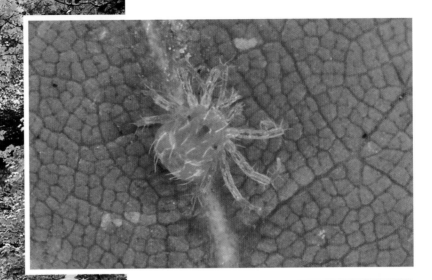

In most of North America, they feed from spring through fall. In tropical areas, chiggers bite all year.

From Egg to Adult

A female adult mite lays eggs on the ground. The larva hatches from the egg one to two weeks later. The chigger crawls to the top of a nearby blade of grass or a fallen leaf. It waits there until a host passes by. When the host brushes against the vegetation, the chigger climbs aboard.

Using its claws, the chigger attaches to the host's skin. The parasite usually chooses the skin inside the ears of furry mammals or around the eyes of birds. On humans, it attaches to tender, moist skin. It stays on the skin surface and does not burrow inside.

Feeding Time

To get its meal, the chigger bites into the skin using its bladelike mouthparts. Its saliva dissolves skin cells, allowing the parasite to feast on the cells' juices.

The parasite stays in the same spot on the host for the entire time it feeds. It does not make a new bite or move to another host.

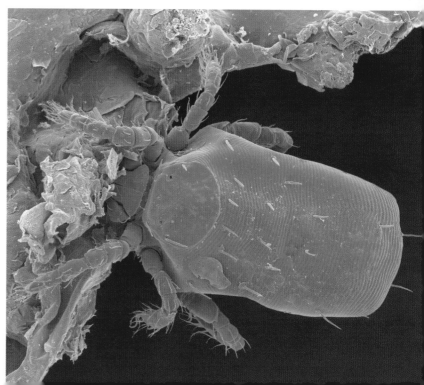

A hungry chigger sinks its bladelike mouthparts into the skin of a human host.

Adult mites, like this bee mite (left), invade the
bodies and legs of insects and bugs.

Feeding can take from several hours to several days. When the chigger is full, it drops
from its host. This will be the chigger's only
meal.

About ten days after dropping to the ground, the chigger develops into an eight-legged mite **nymph**. The nymph eats the bodies and eggs of insects and other hard-shelled soil animals. After two to four weeks, the nymph develops into an adult mite that eats this same diet. Depending on weather conditions, the life cycle from egg to adult takes from forty to seventy-five days.

During warm weather, females lay eggs daily for several weeks. In climates with cold winters, the adult mites spend the winter in the soil or in protected areas near the ground. Females lay eggs again the next spring. In tropical climates, mites reproduce throughout the year.

An Invisible Attacker

Chiggers are so small that five could fit on the period at the end of this sentence. Without a magnifying glass, you probably will not spot one on your skin. But you will know soon enough that it has picked you for its meal.

CHAPTER 2

Attack on Humans

Out of twelve hundred chigger species found throughout the world, only twenty species are known to use humans as hosts. The parasite's attack begins when a person brushes against vegetation where the chigger is waiting.

As the human passes by, the chigger falls onto shoes, pant legs, or exposed skin. Then the parasite begins its search for warm, moist skin that is tender enough to bite. Chigger bites often occur beneath underwear bands, around ankles, in armpits, or in skin creases.

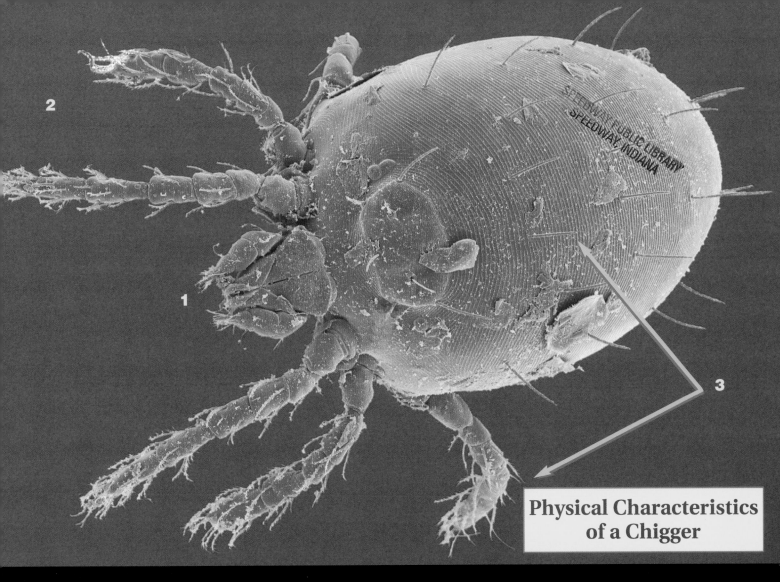

Physical Characteristics of a Chigger

1. The chigger uses its bladelike

2. Six legs and strong claws help

3. Chiggers vary in color from red to

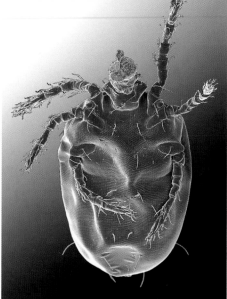

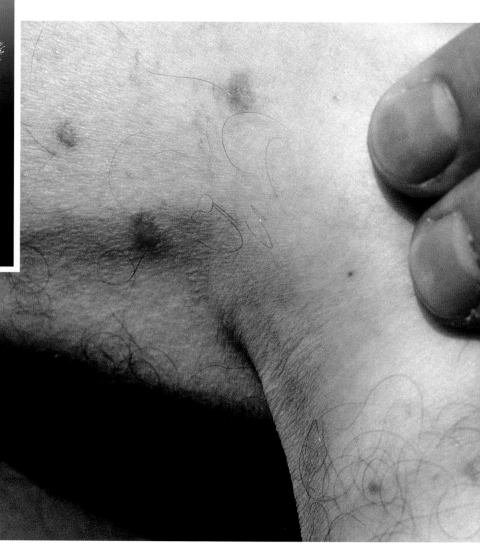

Chemicals in the chigger's saliva dissolve skin cells and cause itchy welts (right).

Once the chigger finds a soft spot on the person's body, it uses its mouthparts to pierce the skin at a pore or **hair follicle**. The person will not be able to feel the tiny chigger as it crawls across the skin or when it bites.

The Body Reacts

The chigger's saliva dissolves the host's skin cells. The human body reacts to chigger saliva by forming a tube of hardened skin at the bite spot. The chigger uses this tube like a straw to suck up the juices from the dissolved skin cells.

Three to six hours after the chigger bites into the skin, the person will feel itching at the bite spot. A **welt**, or swollen skin, appears soon after. The itchy welt is the result of the body's **allergic reaction** to the chemicals in the chigger's saliva. Some people have a more intense reaction to chigger saliva than others do. For them, the itching and swelling is more severe and may last longer.

By the time a person feels the itch, it is too late to stop the chigger's attack. The parasite is already feasting on dissolved skin cells. It eats until it is full, then drops off the person's body. The feeding may last up to three or four days. Scratching by the host often knocks the chigger off before it finishes its meal.

Do Not Be Fooled

The swollen skin and the feeding tube can fool people into thinking that they see the chigger on their skin. But the parasite is so tiny that a person probably will not be able to see it. Besides, it is likely that the chigger has already dropped off or been scratched away.

People sometimes find more than one itchy chigger bite on the body, such as a line of bites around the waist or ankles. Mistakenly, they think that one chigger has taken fresh bites as it moved across the skin. In fact, a chigger only bites once. Each bite in the line is caused by a separate chigger.

It is not unusual for a person to be attacked by several of the parasites at once. Chiggers often sit

in clusters on vegetation as they wait for a host to pass by. Many may jump aboard the host's body together.

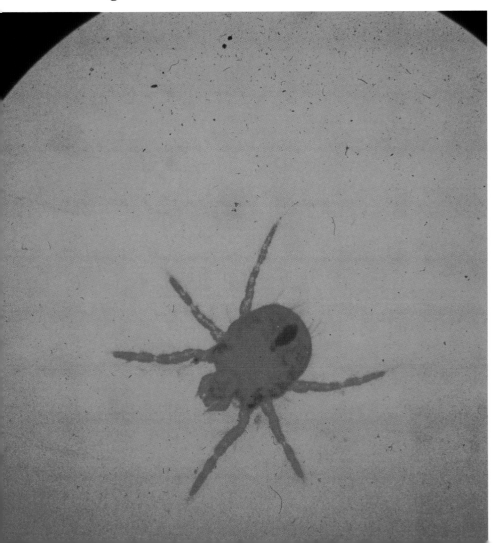

Chiggers are very tiny, even when seen through a microscope.

Nothing to Worry About

Chigger bites in North America do not usually threaten a person's health. The swelling and itch go away in a week or two without any special medical treatment. People sometimes develop skin infections, however, if they scratch open their chigger bites.

While North American chiggers do not cause illness, it is a different story in Asia, where chiggers carry a dangerous and sometimes deadly disease.

CHAPTER 3

The Chigger Disease

In Asia and the Pacific Islands, chigger bites may lead to an illness that includes fever, skin rash, and lung infection. The sickness can last for more than two weeks and is sometimes fatal.

Small and Dangerous

The Japanese call this illness **tsutsugamushi disease**. *Tsutsugamushi* means "small and dangerous creature." The disease is caused by **bacteria** carried to humans by chiggers.

17

The bacterium, *Orientia tsutsugamushi*, is usually found in rodents such as rats and mice. When a chigger feeds on an infected rodent, bacteria enter the chigger's body. As the chigger grows into an adult mite, the bacteria multiply. The female adult mite passes these bacteria to her eggs. Larvae (chiggers) hatch from these eggs carrying the bacteria. If one of the infected chiggers bites a human, it passes the bacteria on to the person.

Adult mites can spread bacteria that cause serious illness in humans.

A Wartime Problem

During World War II, tsutsugamushi disease was a serious problem for soldiers fighting in the Pacific. Thousands of American and British soldiers became ill. The soldiers called tsutsugamushi disease **scrub typhus** because they caught the disease in **scrub** vegetation where rats lived. To control the disease, soldiers killed chiggers by using insecticide on their clothing, bodies, and the ground.

Today, **antibiotic** medicines are available that cure scrub typhus if given in time. But because the

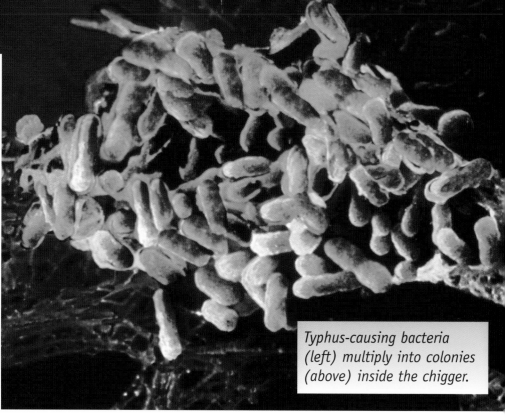

Typhus-causing bacteria (left) multiply into colonies (above) inside the chigger.

illness has symptoms similar to other diseases, doctors do not always recognize it in time. The disease continues to be a problem in Asia.

A Mysterious Fever

In rural Korea, a seventy-two-year-old woman developed a fever and muscle aches. She thought

that she would feel better soon and did not rush to a doctor. When she began to have trouble breathing nearly two weeks later, she finally went to a hospital.

Doctors found a black-crusted sore on the woman's chest. This type of sore at a chigger bite site often indicates scrub typhus. Blood tests proved that she had the disease. For two weeks her doctors gave her antibiotics to fight the scrub typhus bacteria. Unfortunately, the woman's lungs were already so damaged that she died.

Scrub Typhus Down Under

Scrub typhus was not common in the part of northern Australia where a thirty-eight-year-old man was working. That fact cost him his life.

While building tourist paths in the rain forest, the man became ill. He developed a headache, sore throat, cough, fever, and sweats. Thinking that the illness would pass, the man waited to visit a doctor. When he did not improve after a week, he sought medical care. Never suspecting scrub typhus, the local doctor gave him medicine that did not help.

After his symptoms grew worse, the man went to a hospital. Doctors there found a black sore on his lower back that looked typical of scrub typhus. They immediately gave the seriously ill man the antibiotic that kills the scrub typhus bacteria. It was too late. His major organs failed, and he died six days after entering the hospital.

An Uninvited Guest

In some parts of the world, a chigger's bite may carry disease to humans. Regardless of whether a chigger is dangerous or just annoying, most people would rather not be a host to this tiny parasite.

CHAPTER 4

Avoiding Chigger Bites

Chiggers are hard to avoid during warm weather, especially in some parts of North America. Any trip outside, even into the backyard, might expose a person to the tiny creatures. But following some simple tips can help reduce the risk of chigger bites.

Keep Them Away

A good way to keep the parasites off is to stay away from weeds, overgrown grass, and leaf litter where chiggers are most numerous. If it is not possible to

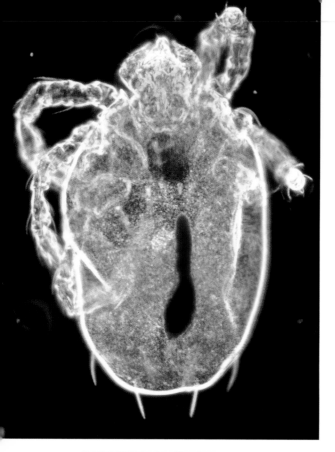

Although chiggers are hard to see, there are ways to avoid the tiny parasites.

avoid these areas, a person should not lie or sit directly on the ground. Sitting on a blanket or chair can stop chiggers from crawling onto the body. Afterward, shaking out the blanket will dislodge any hitchhiking chiggers.

Dressing carefully can protect skin from the parasites. Boots or closed-toe shoes work better than sandals at keeping chiggers off feet. Covering the legs with long pants tucked into socks prevents chiggers from climbing up inside the pant leg.

Some people use chemicals such as DEET to repel chiggers. Like any chemical, DEET must be used carefully, especially around children. It should only be put on clothing, not directly on the skin.

Get Them Off

Even if chiggers have climbed aboard, there is still time to get them off the skin. That is because chiggers may wander over the body for several hours before biting.

Since a chigger is so tiny, it is difficult to spot one. The best way to be sure no chiggers are crawling on the body is to wash all clothing and skin. As

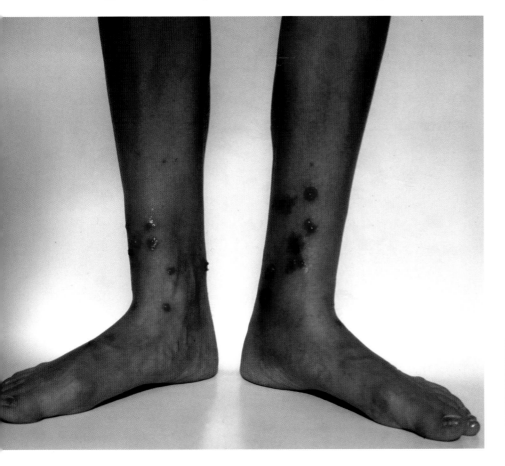

Chigger bites leave itchy welts on a man's ankles. Wearing long pants tucked into socks is one way to prevent chigger bites.

soon as possible, clothes should be removed and shaken—outside the house. Then the clothes should be washed in hot, soapy water before being worn again. Rubbing down the body with a towel or scrubbing the skin in a hot, soapy shower can knock off hitchhiking chiggers.

When a Chigger Attacks

Despite these precautions, a chigger might still find its way to a tender area of skin. A few hours after the chigger bites, the person will feel the itch. Once the body reacts to the chigger's saliva, nothing can shorten the time it takes for the itchy welt to go away.

There are ways, however, to relieve the itch. Some methods are calamine lotion, a baking soda paste, or anti-itch creams. By reducing the itchiness, a person will be less likely to scratch. A scratched-open bite can become infected.

Painting the welt with nail polish or petroleum jelly does not speed the cure by killing the chigger. The chigger is probably not even on the

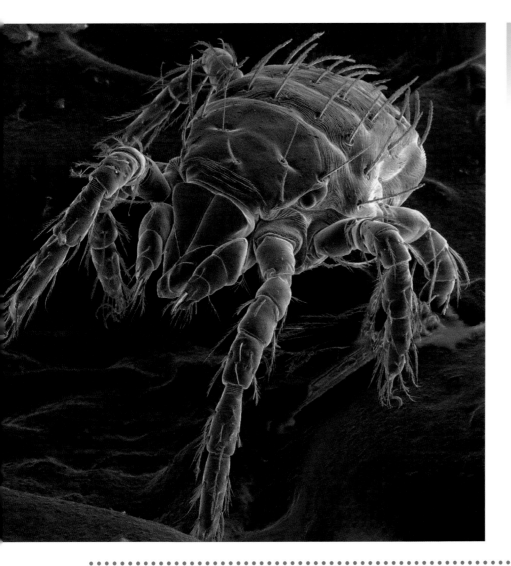

Although some chiggers transmit disease, most chigger bites do not cause serious health problems.

 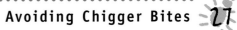

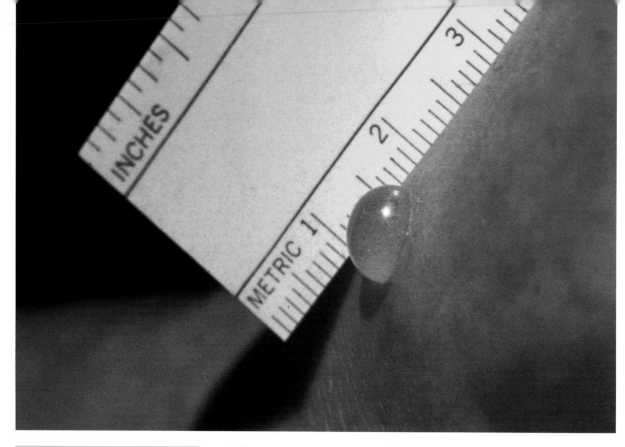

Chigger bites like this one can be painful and itchy.

skin anymore, especially if the person has scratched the spot. The only thing nail polish or petroleum jelly does is keep air away from the welt, which might make it feel less itchy.

With or without special treatment, the chigger bite will heal in a week or two.

 **Chiggers**

A Parasite with Bite

A chigger may be tiny, but its bite makes people feel extremely uncomfortable. Fortunately, most chigger bites do not cause serious health problems. In places where chiggers carry scrub typhus, the disease can usually be cured with antibiotics. A person can avoid many days of itching by knowing where chiggers live and how to get them off the skin before they bite.

allergic reaction: The body's response when it is sensitive to a foreign substance.

antibiotic: A chemical that kills bacteria.

arachnids: The group of eight-legged animals including spiders, scorpions, ticks, and mites.

bacteria: Microscopic organisms; some kinds of bacteria cause disease in humans.

hair follicle: Small pits in the skin from which hair grows.

larva: Also called a chigger; the first stage of a mite's development into an adult after hatching from an egg.

nymph: The second stage of a mite's development into an adult after hatching from an egg.

scrub: An area where short trees, bushes, and shrubs grow close together.

scrub typhus: A disease carried by chiggers in Asia.

tsutsugamushi disease: The Japanese name for scrub typhus.

welt: A swelling that forms at the spot where a chigger bit into the skin.

Internet Sources

Nina Bicknese, "Chiggers!" Missouri Department of Conservation. www.conservation.state.mo.us. A biologist discusses chiggers and explains why most chigger folklore is wrong.

"Chiggers," University of Maryland Home and Garden Information. www.agnr.umd.edu. Gives general information about chigger bites. Click on highlighted words to see photos of mite eggs, larvae, nymphs, and adults.

William F. Lyon, "Chiggers," Ohio State University Extension. http://ohioline. osu.edu. A fact sheet includes details about the chigger mite's life cycle, habitat, and food. Provides advice for avoiding chigger bites.

Kim Rutherford and Dale Schrum, "Hey! A Chigger Bit Me!" KidsHealth for Kids. www.kidshealth.org. This article, written especially for kids, describes what doctors say about chigger bites.

"Scrub Typhus," Dr. Joseph F. Smith Medical Library. www.chclibrary.org. Learn about the symptoms of scrub typhus and how doctors diagnose and treat the disease.